WELCOME TO BOTHWELL CASTLE

Bothwell is one of Scotland's most impressive medieval castles. As early as 1795 it was being hailed as 'the most magnificent ruin in Scotland'. It has suffered down the centuries, but the walls stand yet, monumentally impressive.

The castle was owned by two great noble families. The Murrays created it after acquiring the lordship of Bothwell in 1242. Their plans were never fully realised, and during the Wars of Independence (1296–1356), the castle underwent numerous sieges, the most momentous being Edward I's in 1301. Thirteen years later, on the morning after the Battle of Bannockburn, the pride of England's chivalry was trapped and captured here by the Scots.

After the wars, the Black Douglases became the lords, and impressively rebuilt the castle. Following their downfall in 1455, Bothwell reverted to the Crown and by 1700 it lay abandoned.

Above: The donjon, or keep, seen from the courtyard.

Opposite: Inside the donjon.

CONTENTS

BUILDING SIGHTS

8-11 THE DONJON

The once-mighty keep was partly dismantled in 1337 but was clearly both sophisticated and supremely well-defended.

14 THE SE TOWER

Now the castle's most complete building, this attractive residential tower was added in the early 1400s.

15 THE GREAT HALL

A well-proportioned 15th-century banqueting hall, later enhanced by a row of ten windows.

FINE DETAILS

9 THE CROSSLET ARROWSLITS

Among the many defences arrayed against attackers of the donjon are these versatile archery positions.

13 THE 'COAT-HANGER' DRAWBRIDGE

An ingenious deterrent for intruders, this feature has long outlasted the 14th-century tower it was built to protect.

16 THE PISCINA

This delicately carved receptacle for use at mass is one of few surviving relics of the 15th-century chapel.

BOTHWELL CASTLE AT A GLANCE

Bothwell is really two castles in one. The original castle was built in the later 13th century by the Murrays. Walter Murray and his son, William 'the Rich', planned a mighty castle, far exceeding anything then existing in Scotland.

No matter that they never completed it. What they did achieve was the great circular donjon, or keep. This was justifiably described by the antiquarian W.D. Simpson as, 'the grandest piece of secular architecture that the Middle Ages have bequeathed to us in Scotland', and it still holds us enthralled to this day.

The castle was severely damaged during the Wars of Independence. Thereafter it fell to the new owners, the Black Douglases, to rebuild it. In the 14th and 15th centuries, the 3rd Earl and 4th Earl reconstructed the stronghold. Much of what the visitor sees today is their work, including most of the curtain wall, and the great hall.

THE RESIDENTS

20-27 THE MURRAYS
Though they never completed it, the Murrays planned a castle of magnificent proportions. Ultimately, they were instrumental in its partial destruction.

22-26 THE ENGLISH OCCUPIERS
Bothwell was repeatedly captured, lost and recaptured by English raiders, including Edward I and his grandson Edward III.

28-31 THE BLACK DOUGLASES
Archibald 'the Grim', 3rd Earl of Douglas, acquired Bothwell in 1362. He and his son restored some of its glories, adding many features of their own.

BEYOND THE WALLS

6 THE GRAND PLAN
Remnants to the north of the castle survive as evidence of the ambitious original plan.

19 THE RIVER
The castle commands superb views over the Clyde as it winds towards Glasgow and the sea.

A SHORT TOUR OF BOTHWELL CASTLE

The guided tour on the following pages explores the contributions of the Murrays and Douglases separately. This brief description offers an overview of the whole complex.

1 OUTER WORKS (1200s)
Stone foundations of a curtain wall (never completed), a main gatehouse facing north, small latrine towers to either side, and a round tower housing a well. A wide ditch surrounds it on the outside.

2 GATEHOUSE (SITE OF) (later 1300s)
Entrance into the Douglas castle, demolished around 1700. (The present wall was built in 1987).

3 DONJON (KEEP) (1200s)
The Murrays' private residence, partially demolished after the 1337 siege, and subsequently repaired by the Douglases to become service accommodation.

4 PRISON TOWER (1200s)
Three-storey tower with a prison cell at ground level and a grim pit-prison in the basement.

5 POSTERN (1200s; rebuilt 1300s)
Back (service) gate, defended by a portcullis. Note the stone shield above the door on the outside, which features the Douglas coat of arms.

6 LATRINE TOWER (early 1400s)
Served the noble apartments in the adjacent south range.

7 SOUTH RANGE (early 1400s)
Little is left of this once-elegant, two-storey domestic range. It probably served as the 4th Earl of Douglas's lodging, and was occupied well into the 17th century.

8 CHAPEL (early 1400s)
On the first floor above a ground-floor cellar, the chapel's once-spacious interior was lit by three tall windows in the south wall. Traces remain of a vaulted ceiling, a bench for the officiating priests, a piscina, a sacrament house and a holy-water basin.

9 SE TOWER (early 1400s)
Crowned with attractive machicolations (corbelled-out, slotted parapets), this tower's upper storeys housed private chambers.

10 GREAT HALL (early 1400s)
On the first floor above three stone-vaulted cellars, this was the main banqueting and reception room of the Douglas castle. The row of windows in the west (courtyard) wall was perhaps inserted around 1500, at James IV's command. The fireplace in the north cellar may date from the English occupation of the 1330s.

11 TOWER HOUSE (SITE OF) (later 1300s)
Built by Archibald 'the Grim' to replace lordly accommodation in the donjon, the tower house was largely demolished around 1700. It has remains of a most unusual 'coat-hanger' drawbridge in its first-floor entrance.

12 KITCHENS (SITE OF) (later 1300s/1400s)
Remains of a fireplace and oven (above the site manager's office and shop) indicate the position of kitchens serving the adjacent great hall.

THE CASTLE OF THE MURRAYS

Today, Bothwell Castle is very different from the complex planned by its creator in the 1200s. We do not know how much of the original scheme was completed, but clearly a mighty stone stronghold was envisaged, covering more than twice the area of the present castle. Had the Murray castle been completed, it would without doubt have been the most spectacular castle in Scotland and one of the premier castles in western Europe.

THE CURTAIN WALLS AND GATEHOUSE

The original castle was planned as a great courtyard castle covering over 0.75 hectares (1.8 acres) and surrounded by a high, thick enclosure wall. Projecting from this curtain wall were even loftier towers, all but one circular on plan. Rectangular latrine towers, serving buildings behind the curtain wall, also appeared at intervals. Encircling the curtain wall was a great ditch.

The courtyard, or close, was entered via two gateways. The principal entrance was an impressive and well-defended gatehouse on the north side. This comprised two large round towers projecting out from the curtain wall and flanking a central entrance passage. In front of the passage was a drawbridge, of which the stone-lined drawbridge pit remains. The second entrance was a postern, or back-gate, in the south curtain wall, for use by servants and workmen.

By analogy with other castles, we can guess that the gatehouse provided living quarters in its upper floors for the constable, or keeper of the castle, who was responsible for security. The Murray family's own suite of rooms was within the great circular donjon at the west side. The upper floors of the lesser towers provided accommodation for other senior members of the lord's huge household above store-rooms at ground level. The prison tower beside the postern evidently included prison cells, and the tower to the west of the gatehouse housed a well. The courtyard itself enclosed other important buildings. These included a great hall, for banquets and gatherings of the baron court, a chapel, kitchens, bakehouse and brewhouse. All these have long since disappeared.

Opposite : A reconstruction drawing of 1957 shows the Murray castle as it might have looked if the full grand scheme had ever been completed.

Above: The prison tower and the postern gate.

Below: Remnants of the original gatehouse.

Excavations in the 1930s, together with evidence from the upstanding architecture and the surviving documentary record, combine to suggest that building work did not get far. The great donjon, its wing walls and enclosing moat were completed, as was the adjacent prison tower. Foundations were laid for the curtain wall, the gatehouse and the remaining towers.

THE DONJON

The great circular donjon served as the Murrays' private residence, capable of being independently defended if the remainder of the castle fell into enemy hands. Before its partial destruction in 1337 it was almost 20m in diameter with walls nearly 5m thick. It still stands over 27m high.

THE DONJON AS DEFENCE

The donjon's various defensive features are still readily identifiable. First there is the moat, now dry but originally filled with water. The sluice opening, for draining away the water, is visible at the base of the wall to the left of the donjon. This sluice was sited directly beneath the donjon's latrines so that the outflowing water could flush them.

Key

1 Corbels to support a defensive gallery
2 Lord's private chamber
3 Raggle for roof of wall-walk
4 Wall-walk
5 Put-log holes for scaffolding
   (used during construction)
6 Beak
7 Lord's hall
8 Crosslet arrowslits
9 Holes for drawbridge chains
10 Entrance to donjon
11 Moat
12 Sluice

The two wing walls on either side of the donjon have parapet walks at their top, from where the defenders could fire down on raiders. The triangular-shaped raggles (grooves) for the roofs covering these walks are clearly visible on the donjon.

The courtyard wall of the donjon has an angular projection on its north side. This 'beak' turned the entrance away from the open courtyard, making it harder for an enemy to use a battering-ram to smash down the doors. The entrance itself is a fine pointed doorway. It was originally reached by a timber bridge across the moat, with a drawbridge connecting the bridge to the entrance. Holes for the chains that lifted the bridge can be seen above the doorway. When the drawbridge was raised, it was recessed into the beak to serve as an extra barrier. Immediately inside the entrance was a portcullis: the vertical slots by which it was raised and lowered are visible on either side of the door. Beyond was a zig-zagged passage that would also hinder an enemy.

A little higher up the beak are two crosslet arrowslits, for use by defenders stationed in the room housing the drawbridge and portcullis lifting apparatus. Above the entrance, at the top of the donjon, was a box-like stone structure projecting out from the wall. Openings in its floor enabled the defenders to protect the entrance below; some of the stone corbels supporting it remain.

Top left: The donjon, seen from the courtyard.

Top centre: One of the crosslet arrow slits covering the courtyard.

Top right: Access from the donjon to the wall-walk, which was once covered by a steep pitched roof.

THE DONJON AS RESIDENCE

The accommodation within the donjon was spread over four floors. We cannot be certain how the Murrays used them but, as a rule, the more private and exclusive accommodation was on the higher levels.

The entrance passage leads into the first-floor room. This was probably the lord's hall, a more restricted reception chamber to complement the great hall (now gone) in the courtyard. Because of its partial destruction in 1337, the original octagonal-shaped room has been reduced to less than half its size, thus losing much of its grandeur. A handsome traceried window with stone side-benches in its wide bay still gives fine views over the courtyard to the east, but the missing walls on the west surely housed another, as well as an impressive fireplace.

Right: The interior of the donjon as it may have looked when complete.

DID YOU KNOW . . .

The architect of the donjon cleverly contrived to provide a secret escape route for the lord. Access to the parapet-walk on top of the south wing wall is reached only from his bedchamber at the top of the donjon, thus enabling him to reach the prison tower and so, by way of its external stair, the postern – and safety.

A fine pointed arcade of stone ribs ran round the walls. The ceiling was evidently a wooden vault supported in part by the central stone pillar that can be seen rising from the basement. The doorway to the right of the window leads to the latrine closet. A second doorway, to the left of the entrance door, gives access to the spiral stair linking all four floors.

The basement was clearly used for storage. Aside from the once-central stone pier (now immured in a crude wall added by the Douglases), all that remains is the well, 6m deep, beside which is a recess for the bucket. Incised into the wall beside the well is a ducal coronet over the initial B and date 1786 – thought to be graffiti left by the 3rd Duke of Buccleuch.

The floor above the lord's hall is relatively featureless today, making its use difficult to establish. The passage in the south wall leading to a second latrine closet confirms that the chamber was intended for residential use.

The top floor was almost certainly the lord's private chamber. This has also been a handsome room, with a fine, traceried window facing onto the courtyard. Here too we are missing the fireplace and perhaps another west-facing window.

Neither of these upper floors was vaulted. Instead, they had strongly strutted ceilings, indicated by joist-pockets, projecting corbels and narrow vertical recesses. The roof above the top chamber provided the lord with fine views over his lands, as well as a fighting platform for his men in time of need.

Top: Carved graffiti in the donjon basement, possibly left by Henry Scott, 3rd Duke of Buccleuch and chairman of the Royal Bank of Scotland.

Above: One of the arched doorways leading into the stairway.

THE CASTLE OF THE DOUGLASES

When Archibald 'the Grim' became lord of Bothwell in 1362, he found the castle in a very dilapidated state, especially the great donjon, partly destroyed by Sir Andrew Murray in 1337. He began a major rebuilding programme which continued until his death in 1400 and was carried on by his son, Archibald, the 4th Earl. Their combined endeavours transformed the castle.

ARCHIBALD THE GRIM'S CONTRIBUTION

Archibald the Grim abandoned the donjon as the lord's private residence within the castle and replaced it with a new rectangular tower at the opposite end of the courtyard, where he and Lady Joanna could reside in modern comfort. The tower house was one of the first of its type to be built in Scotland. The donjon was crudely repaired, perhaps to serve as quarters for the Douglases' extensive household of retainers and servants.

Top: The castle as it may have looked around 1420.

Above: The coat of arms of Archibald the Grim.

Below left: The Douglas arms carved above the postern gate.
Below centre: The remnants of Archibald the Grim's tower house.
Below right: The 'coat hanger' drawbridge protecting the tower house's first-floor entrance.

Bottom right:
A drawing by MacGibbon & Ross shows how the drawbridge operated.

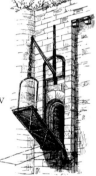

The donjon and tower house were linked by a new and formidable stone curtain wall, most of which still survives. It enclosed an area less than half the size of the castle complex planned by the Murrays, but was nonetheless substantial. The courtyard was entered through a new gatehouse at the centre of the north side. This large rectangular tower was demolished around 1700 and its stone used in constructing the new mansion nearby. However, with the help of John Slezer's engraving of 1693 (see page 30) and John Lewis's excavations in 1981 we have a reasonably good idea of its footprint and height.

The present grassed courtyard seems to have been divided into two courts, or closes, of roughly equal size. The west close would have been the outer, or service, close, where the retainers and servants went about their business. These menials continued to use the old postern in the south wall. The inner close to the east was for the exclusive use of the Douglas family and their honoured guests. Their visitors would have entered via the gatehouse on the north wall. They would have encountered buildings ranged around all four sides of the close, with Archibald the Grim's great tower looming over all from the NE corner.

Little remains of these buildings, though their stone footings lurk beneath the present green sward. The biggest loss is Archibald's tower. It seems to have been even grander than his other great tower at Threave in Galloway. What little remains suggests that it was something a bit special – most notably the 'coat-hanger' imprint of the drawbridge that protected the tower's first-floor entrance.

THE 4TH EARL'S CONTRIBUTION

I t is impossible now to determine what Archibald the Grim managed to build prior to his death in 1400. It is clear from the surviving architecture that his son, Archibald, the 4th Earl, completed what his father had started. But it is also likely that he radically altered it.

We can deduce that the son completed his father's work from the machicolated (slotted) parapet overhanging the wallhead of the SE tower. This attractive defensive feature can date from no earlier than the early 1400s. It suggests that the son was topping off his father's curtain wall in the latest style – one he'd no doubt seen on his extensive travels on the Continent.

Above: One of numerous decorated ceramic jugs found at Bothwell, probably dating from the Douglas era.

Left: The SE tower. The distinctive parapet at the top shows that this building was not completed until the early 1400s.

Opposite: Inside the great hall, around 1420.

THE GREAT HALL

The great hall provides clear evidence that the 4th Earl departed from his father's vision. Its location shows that it was not built at the same time as the NE tower. The elaborate 'coat-hanger' drawbridge protecting the tower's entrance would not have been able to operate. The other oddity is the location of the dais window at the top end of the hall, where the lord and his guests sat. This is at the SW corner, the furthest point from the NE tower. These clues suggest that the son downgraded his father's tower and built a new private residence along the south range.

The great hall is on the first floor, above three stone-vaulted cellars. It was reached by a timber stair from the courtyard. There may have been a timber gallery running along the courtyard wall at first-floor level. Two doors gave access into the great hall. The wider door at the north end was the public entrance. There are signs in the stonework inside the hall that a timber partition screened off this 'lower' end, and that there was a minstrels' gallery above. The narrower door at the south end was for the use of the Douglases and their guests. Next to it is the fine traceried dais window. The hall had no fireplace and was probably heated by free-standing braziers.

OTHER ADDITIONS OF THE 4TH EARL

The two-storey lodging along the south range was a more practical residence than the NE tower, with fewer stairs. It was also on the sunnier side of the castle, with fine views over the Clyde. But only tantalising glimpses of it remain.

Surviving features include fine south-facing windows, and remains of partition walls and doorways. The latrine tower at its SW corner still remains largely complete. Discarded tiles, pots and candlesticks were found in its cesspit.

The once fine chapel to the east comprised three bays, each lit by a tall lancet window. Part of the vaulted ceiling survives, as does a stone bench along the south wall, raised at the east end where the clergy sat. Other features include the sacrament house and piscina at the east end, and a holy-water stoup at the west end, where the elite congregation cleansed their hands.

The adjacent SE tower housed a storage basement and three upper chambers, each with a fireplace and privy. It is tempting to see this tower occupied by the earl's clerk, responsible for all his spiritual and secretarial needs.

LATER ALTERATIONS

Following the overthrow of the Black Douglases in 1455, Bothwell became a royal castle. From time to time, alterations were made to make the place fit for the king's visits.

Two obvious modifications are visible. The first is in the great hall, where ten slender windows were inserted into the west wall. These date from the early 1500s, and were probably installed at the behest of either James IV or James V. They are strikingly similar to the so-called 'ladder window' in the King's Presence Chamber at Linlithgow Palace, dating from the 1530s.

The second alteration is in the south range, where the curtain wall has been heightened and fine transomed windows inserted. One of the windows had a timber balcony projecting out from it which must have provided an even better vista of the surrounding countryside. Once again the hand of James IV or James V is suspected.

Far left: The latrine tower and fine windows are all that remain of the south range.

Left: The arched windows of the chapel, next to the SE tower.

Below: The great hall, with its row of ten windows, added in the early 1500s.

THE STORY OF
BOTHWELL
CASTLE

Picture: Detail of a drawing by Paul Sandby of the castle from the SW bank of the Clyde. Probably around 1750.

The important medieval lordship of Bothwell was created by the Crown in the mid-1100s and granted to David Olifard, lord of Sawtry, in eastern England. The Olifards remained lords of Bothwell for the next 100 years, and founded the Scottish family of Oliphant.

In 1141, with the power-struggle between King Stephen and Queen Matilda of England at its height, David I of Scotland (1124–53) was helped to escape from the Battle of Winchester by his godson David Olifard, lord of Sawtry, in the Honour of Huntingdon. King David rewarded him with the estate of Smailholm, in Roxburghshire. Later, when David Olifard had his Sawtry lordship confiscated, Malcolm IV (1153–65) bestowed on him the new lordship of Bothwell, beside the River Clyde. (The lordship comprised the land lying between the North and South Calder Water, which join the Clyde on either side of Bothwell Castle.) David Olifard was also given an important position at the Scottish court, most probably as justiciar (chief law officer) of Lothian. His son and grandson, both named Walter, also served as justiciars of Lothian.

We do not know where David Olifard built his castle. It may well have been sited beside the ancient parish church in the town of Bothwell. During restoration work there in the 1930s, several carved stone fragments of 12th-century date were found, confirming that David Olifard or his son had erected a handsome church to complement their castle.

TIMELINE

1141	AROUND 1611

DAVID OLIFARD
lord of Sawtry, Lincolnshire, helps David I of Scotland escape from Battle of Winchester.

MALCOLM IV
grants David Olifard the rich lordship of Bothwell.

BOTHWELL AND THE MURRAYS

When Walter Olifard (II), grandson of David Olifard, died in 1242, the lordship of Bothwell passed to his son-in-law, Walter of Moray (Murray). Walter, lord of Petty, near Inverness, soon moved south to his wife's richer barony.

The present castle was most probably begun by Walter Murray, and continued by his son William. Walter was lord of Petty, east of Inverness, where his modest motte-and-bailey castle can still be seen. His marriage into the Olifard family raised him to the highest rank in noble society. He even inherited the prestigious post of justiciar of Lothian from his father-in-law.

He made sure everyone knew. The mighty stone castle he began building was a visible statement of his newly-exalted status in society. It was conceived on the grand scale. Its huge, polygonal curtain wall enclosed an area covering 0.75 hectares (1.8 acres). This put it on a par with Edward I of England's mighty Caernarfon, in North Wales, and far ahead of its Scottish contemporaries, for example Kildrummy and Caerlaverock.

We do not know when Walter embarked on his building venture, though a date after 1270 is suggested by the surviving architecture. The great project was continued by his son, William, who succeeded him in 1278.

Left: A gravestone in St Bride's Church, Bothwell, thought to be the monument of Walter of Moray.

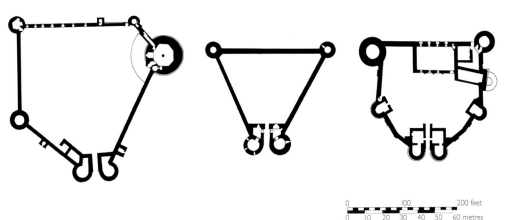

Above: Scale diagram showing the footprint of (left) Bothwell Castle as it was originally planned, alongside its Scottish contemporaries Caerlaverock Castle (centre) and Kildrummy Castle (right).

William was known as 'le Riche' on account of his great wealth, and it is possible that he earned his nickname, in part at least, because of his extravagant residence, which was without equal in Scotland.

William the Rich seems never to have seen his great castle completed. Archaeological excavations in the 1930s suggested that construction of the twin-towered gatehouse and adjacent lengths of curtain wall never got any higher than the foundations. It is highly likely that the outbreak of the Wars of Independence in 1296 brought an abrupt halt to proceedings.

1242

WALTER OF MORAY
marries into the Olifard family and becomes lord of Bothwell. He abandons Petty Castle for the more prosperous south.

AROUND 1270

WALTER
begins building the present castle.

BOTHWELL IN THE WARS OF INDEPENDENCE

Mighty Bothwell Castle naturally figured prominently in the bloody Wars of Independence against England that dominated the first half of the 1300s. Siege followed on siege, with the result that, following the final siege in 1337, the once-great castle of the Murrays was reduced to a wrecked and burnt-out shell.

Edward I invaded Scotland on 30 March 1296. Four weeks later, at the disastrous Battle of Dunbar, Sir William Murray, lord of Bothwell, was captured and taken south to London. His castle was soon in English hands. William's nephew and heir, Andrew Murray, was also taken at Dunbar. The latter soon escaped from his prison in Chester Castle and returned north to lead the Scottish resistance with William Wallace. This alliance resulted in the Scots' momentous victory at Stirling Bridge in September 1297. Andrew, alas, was mortally wounded in the battle. However, his son, born posthumously and named Andrew in honour of his illustrious father, would one day wreak vengeance on the English at Bothwell Castle.

In 1299, the Scots laid siege to Bothwell. It lasted 14 tedious months before succeeding. The English keeper, Stephen Brampton, later complained to his king that he had defended the castle 'for a year and nine weeks, to his great loss and misfortune' and then languished for three years in a Scottish prison.

THE GREAT SIEGE OF 1301

Bothwell Castle endured several sieges during the Wars of Independence. The most famous occurred during Edward I's summer campaign of 1301, when the castle was in Scottish hands.

By 23 August the English army – 6,800 men, including 20 masons and 20 miners – had reached Cambusnethan, seven miles from Bothwell. Work began on constructing a great siege engine, called 'le berefrey'. (A belfry was a wooden tower on wheels, with a drawbridge at the top that could be dropped onto the battlements of a castle.) On 29 August, the belfry began its ponderous journey to Bothwell, where the siege had already begun. The 'wood of Glasgu' was plundered to provide materials for a bridge over the Clyde and a road to take the awesome machine up to the castle walls.

The siege was over within a month. By 24 September, the belfry was on its way to the siege of Stirling Castle. Edward I left about the same time (he had spent four days at Bothwell, overseeing the final stages). He left the castle in the hands of Aymer de Valence, Earl of Pembroke, a veteran of Stirling Bridge. Pembroke had already been granted the barony of Bothwell by Edward I, in anticipation of a successful outcome. The name 'Valence Tower' has long been applied to the great donjon, where Valence presumably set up his headquarters.

1296

EDWARD I OF ENGLAND besieges and captures Bothwell Castle during his initial invasion of Scotland, which began the long and bloody Wars of Independence.

1301

AYMER DE VALENCE, EARL OF PEMBROKE takes possession of Bothwell following a second major siege by Edward I.

23

BOTHWELL AND BANNOCKBURN, 1314

Bothwell Castle remained firmly in English hands following the 1301 siege. In 1311 it had a garrison of 60 men. But the English hold over Bothwell came to an abrupt end in June 1314, in the immediate aftermath of Robert Bruce's great victory at Bannockburn.

After the 1301 siege, the English king ensured Bothwell was well garrisoned. As one of the greatest castles in central Scotland, it had an important role to play in the continuing conflict. In 1311, Sir Walter FitzGilbert de Hameldone, its keeper, had a 60-strong garrison, including 28 knights and 29 archers. The last entry in the English records before Bannockburn, for 8 February 1312, records Edward II instructing FitzGilbert, a Scot fighting on the English side, to see that the castle 'is safely and securely kept, and delivered to no other person whatsoever without the king's letter patent under the Great Seal of England directed to himself'. This hints at Edward's anxiety, aroused by Bruce's rapid progress. His concern soon proved well founded.

Left: An illustration of the Battle of Bannockburn, from Walter Bower's *Scotichronicon* (1447).

DID YOU KNOW . . .

Walter FitzGilbert de Hameldone, the Scot holding Bothwell for King Edward II of England at the time of Bannockburn, surrendered his charge the day after the battle. He somehow survived his treachery to become the ancestor of the powerful Hamilton family.

Over two days in June 1314, Bruce's army overwhelmed and humiliated Edward's far superior force at Bannockburn. In the chaos that brought the second day (Monday 24 June) to a close, the surviving English knights did their utmost to get back to England. As Edward galloped SE to Dunbar, his joint-commander, Humphrey de Bohun, Earl of Hereford, sped SW to Bothwell with a considerable cavalry force, reaching the castle late that same night. When they awoke the following morning they found themselves trapped, for King Robert's brother Edward Bruce and his men had tracked them across country and laid siege to Bothwell. FitzGilbert, still the castle's keeper, realised all was lost and surrendered his charge. Bruce made full use of the large ransoms available, for sheltering in the castle, besides Hereford, were Robert de Umfraville, Earl of Angus, Maurice, lord of Berkeley, John, lord of Segrave and others. Hereford alone was exchanged for Bruce's queen Elizabeth, his sister Mary, his daughter Marjorie, and old Robert Wishart, Bishop of Glasgow.

In accordance with Bruce's usual policy, the castle was rendered militarily useless. An English chronicler, referring to a later occupation of the castle by Edward III, records that the English found it in ruins, 'having been formerly destroyed by the Scots'.

Above: A headless effigy in Glasgow Cathedral, thought to represent Bishop Robert Wishart, who supported Robert Bruce during the Wars of Independence.

Below: The coat of arms of Humphrey de Bohun, Earl of Hereford, captured at Bothwell by Edward Bruce.

1314

KING ROBERT BRUCE
routs Edward II's superior forces at the Battle of Bannockburn.

1314

EDWARD BRUCE
brother of King Robert I, recaptures Bothwell on the morning after Bannockburn and takes prisoner many English knights.

BOTHWELL'S LAST SIEGE, 1337

The final siege of Bothwell brought to an end a short English occupation, which included a brief stay by Edward III. Within three months of the king's departure, Sir Andrew Murray, lord of Bothwell, arrived at his ancestral castle.

The coronation of Edward Balliol, the late King John's son, at Scone in 1332 revived and prolonged the Wars of Independence. By October 1336, Bothwell once again had an English garrison. The castle was evidently damaged because Master John of Kilburne was sent from Edinburgh Castle to carry out repairs. Kilburne was a man of high standing in his craft, and his workmanship may survive at Bothwell, in the fireplace in the north cellar under the early 15th-century great hall.

On 18 November, Edward III made Bothwell his headquarters. But by mid-December it was clear that his position in Scotland was becoming untenable, and he beat a hasty retreat to Newcastle.

The Scotsman most responsible for the reverse was none other than Sir Andrew Murray of Bothwell ('the noble Andrew'), son of the victor of Stirling Bridge 30 years earlier. He was now acting as Guardian of Scotland for the young David II, Bruce's son. By the time Sir Andrew appeared before the walls of his ancestral castle in March 1337, he had already thrown the English out of numerous fortresses north of the Forth. Each recaptured stronghold was destroyed, the strategy previously adopted by Bruce.

Left: A medieval illustration of a castle under siege.

Opposite far right: The coat of arms of Sir Andrew Murray.

During his month-long stay at Bothwell, Edward III (left) issued a number of writs, including orders for the naval protection of the English coast. He also summoned parliament to meet in London to co-ordinate the means for carrying on the war against the Scots and the French.

Sir Andrew Murray made short work of capturing Bothwell, thanks largely to another powerful siege engine called 'Bowstoure' (perhaps a battering-ram), which had previously helped him take St Andrews Castle. Once the castle was taken, Sir Andrew was under patriotic obligation to destroy his own property. He did not hold back. An English chronicler tells us that the castle was 'scattered from the foundations', clearly an exaggeration. But the loss of one half of the great donjon, or keep – 'that stalwart toure' – is almost certainly an act perpetrated by Sir Andrew.

AROUND 1332 | 1337

ENGLISH FORCES
retake Bothwell Castle early in the second War of Independence, in support of the revived Balliol claim to the throne.

SIR ANDREW MURRAY
finally ousts the English and partially demolishes his ancestral home, damaging the mighty donjon.

BOTHWELL AND THE BLACK DOUGLASES

After its dismantling in 1337, the castle lay abandoned until 1362. In that year, Lady Joanna Murray married Archibald Douglas 'the Grim'. Over the next century, Archibald and his heirs restored the castle to something approaching its former glory.

In 1362 Lady Joanna, the wealthy heiress of the Murrays' estates, married Archibald Douglas, illegitimate son of 'the Good Sir James' of Douglas, Robert Bruce's warrior companion. The union brought him 'treasour untald . . . with rent and riches'. The richest treasure was the lordship of Bothwell. It transformed a landless knight into a wealthy nobleman. Already known as 'the Grim', but yet to become Lord of Galloway (1369) and 3rd Earl of Douglas (1388), Archibald quickly set about rebuilding his wife's shattered castle to make it his chief seat. He built several other castles too, most notably the gaunt, forbidding tower on Threave Island, in Galloway. But his favourite residence was Bothwell, and many of his charters were dated and sealed there.

In 1398, Earl Archibald received papal permission to elevate Bothwell parish church into the collegiate church of St Bride's (St Bride was his family's patron saint). There, in 1399, he and Lady Joanna witnessed the marriage of their daughter Elizabeth to Robert III's eldest son, the Duke of Rothesay. Archibald the Grim died the following year at Threave, but his body was laid to rest in St Bride's, Bothwell and not beside his father in the family mausoleum at St Bride's, Douglas. (His tomb, unfortunately, no longer survives.)

Opposite bottom left:
A portrait thought to
show Archibald, 4th Earl
of Douglas.

Opposite bottom right:
An engraving of the castle
dated 1802.

Left: Some of the 13th
or 14th-century ceramic
jugs that were found
during excavations at
Bothwell.

Below: A 15th-century
bronze ewer spout also
found at the site.

His son and heir, Archibald, 4th Earl of Douglas and 1st Duke of
Touraine, continued the rebuilding programme, even though his
preferred main residence was the prestigious royal castle of Edinburgh,
of which he was keeper until his death in 1424. At Bothwell, he made
a number of changes to his father's castle (see pages 14–16). The 4th Earl
was one of Europe's finest warriors, who became Lieutenant-General of
the French king's army. We have no proof, but it is conceivable that he
may have employed the Paris-born master-mason, John Morow, to work
on his Bothwell residence. Certainly, by the time of his death, fighting
the English at the Battle of Verneuil, in France, in 1424, Bothwell Castle
had risen from the ashes to become once again one of the most
impressive noble seats of its day.

1362

**ARCHIBALD
THE GRIM**
marries Joanna
Murray of Bothwell
and takes possession
of the castle, which
he begins rebuilding.

1424

**HIS SON,
THE 4TH EARL**
dies at the Battle of
Verneuil, having completed
the remodelling of
Bothwell Castle.

THE TWILIGHT YEARS

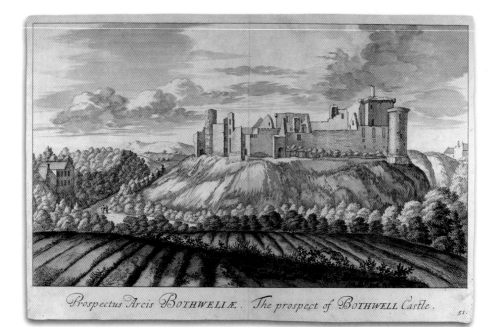

Prospectus Arcis BOTHWELLIÆ. *The prospect of* BOTHWELL *Castle*.

With the downfall of the Black Douglases in 1455, the castle lost much of its greatness. The castle and lordship reverted to the Crown and the castle thereafter passed through a number of noble families in quick succession. In 1492, it was acquired by the Red Douglases, kinsmen of the Black Douglases, but the mighty walls were never to figure again in the nation's history.

In 1455 the Black Douglases were overthrown by James II. Bothwell, along with the rest of their castles, came into Crown possession. It was entrusted to the safe-keeping of several noble families in succession. In 1489 it was bestowed on Patrick Hepburn, 2nd Lord Hailes, whom James IV made 1st Earl of Bothwell. In 1492, at the king's request, Earl Patrick was persuaded to exchange his new seat for Hermitage Castle, in Liddesdale, with Archibald Douglas, 5th Earl of Angus. And so Bothwell passed out of the hands of the Black Douglases and into those of their Red Douglas kinsmen.

Left: An engraving by John Slezer of the castle from the south, dated 1693. At this time, the tower house was still standing at the NE corner of the castle. Bothwell House is also visible at the far right.

James IV (1488–1513) visited the castle on several occasions. During his stays he played cards with the earl, enjoyed a spot of hawking, and was entertained by minstrels. He even purchased pots and tiles there, but for what purpose is not made clear in the Treasurer's Accounts. His son, James V, also incurred expenses at Bothwell, though we do not know how. Certainly, building works were underway at the castle in the early 1500s. Most obvious today is the row of windows inserted into the front wall of the great hall.

But the ancient castle was fast becoming a burden on its noble owners. Finally, towards the end of the 1600s, Archibald Douglas, 1st Earl of Forfar, built a new mansion, confusingly also called Bothwell Castle, a little to the east of the castle. It is said that he pulled down parts of the old castle to provide building stone for his new Palladian mansion, and the non-existence today of Archibald the Grim's great tower and gatehouse may be proof of that. Earl Archibald died in his new 'castle' in 1712, and his widow in 1740. Thereafter, new Bothwell Castle too went into decline. It was eventually demolished in 1926, the victim of subsidence from coalmining. The ancient castle proved far more robust and in 1935 was placed in State care.

Top: James IV, who stayed at Bothwell a number of times.

Above: A pub sign in Bothwell today.

1455

JAMES II overthrows the Black Douglases and Bothwell becomes a royal castle.

AROUND 1700

ARCHIBALD DOUGLAS, 1ST EARL OF FORFAR abandons the old castle for a new mansion nearby. This is demolished in 1926.

Aside from Bothwell Castle, Historic Scotland has many properties around the Clyde. A selection is given below.

GLASGOW CATHEDRAL

The most complete medieval cathedral on the Scottish mainland, still in use nearly 900 years after it was established.

↗ In Glasgow city centre, off the M8

🕐 Open all year

📞 0141 552 6891

🚗 Approx 10 miles from Bothwell Castle

CRAIGNETHAN CASTLE

A dramatically sited, state-of-the-art fortress–residence built to the latest fashions of the 1530s.

↗ 5.5 miles NW of Lanark, off the A72

🕐 Open all year
Winter: weekends only

📞 01555 860 364

🚗 Approx 15 miles from Bothwell Castle

DUMBARTON CASTLE

The ancient stronghold of Strathclyde, which played many roles over centuries of royal and military use

↗ In Dumbarton off the A82

🕐 Open all year
Winter: closed Thu/Fri

📞 01389 732 167

🚗 Approx 30 miles from Bothwell Castle

NEWARK CASTLE

Built in the late 1400s, Newark was transformed a century later into a splendid Renaissance mansion.

↗ In Port Glasgow on the A8 at Newark

🕐 Open summer only

📞 01475 741 858

🚗 Approx 30 miles from Bothwell Castle

For more information on all Historic Scotland sites, visit **www.historic-scotland.gov.uk**
To order tickets and a wide range of gifts, visit **www.historic-scotland.gov.uk/shop**

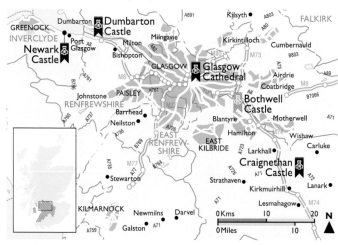

Bus/coach parking	🚌
Car parking	🅿
Interpretive display	
Reasonable wheelchair access	♿
Shop	
Toilets	👫
Self-serve tea and coffee	
Picnic area	
Bicycle rack	
No dogs	⊗